Wheat Free Cooking

Made Easy

Delicious Wheat Free Recipes for the Entire Family!

DISCLAIMER

No part of this eBook can be transmitted or reproduced in any form including print, electronic, photocopying, scanning, mechanical or recording without prior written permission from the author.

While the author has taken utmost efforts to ensure the accuracy of the written content, all readers are advised to follow information mentioned herein at their own risk. The author cannot be held responsible for any personal or commercial damage caused by misinterpretation of information.

All information, ideas, and guidelines presented here are for educational purposes only and readers are encouraged to seek professional advice when needed

SUMMARY

If you are looking for wheat-free recipes, you have chosen just the eBook for it.

It is crucial to know the ground rules for any kind of diet, and if you are looking for wheat free recipes, you can read right through!

Here is a glimpse of what this eBook has in store for you:

- A "Foods that are allowed list" to check which foods are allowed when you are going wheat-free.
- Wheat free recipes with complete step wise, easy-to-follow directions.
- Each recipe has a picture for you to know what you will be cooking.

What is more that you will find:

- Serving size for each recipe
- Cooking time for every recipe
- Nutritional value for every recipe
- Last but not the least, delicious recipes for b**reakfast**, **lunch**, and **dinner**, which are easy to cook, yummy and provide you a meal plan for the entire day.

So what are you waiting for? Scroll down to discover the yummiest wheat free recipes!

Contents

INTRODUCTION

Many people suffer from food allergies, but you do not have to worry about it if you have been diagnosed with a wheat allergy. With a simple knowledge of foods, which are wheat free, you can easily prepare yummy foods, which will cause you no trouble.

Normally people who are allergic to wheat or want to avoid wheat, should also avoid gluten. There are many foods, which are wheat and gluten free. The list is provided below for your easy reference:

FOODS THAT ARE ALLOWED ON WHEAT FREE DIET:

1. Meat
2. Fish
3. Chicken
4. Fruits
5. Vegetables
6. Nuts
7. Legumes
8. Beans

Grains, which you can take:

1. Rice
2. Quinoa
3. Teff
4. Millet
5. Buckwheat
6. Oats

Fats:

1. Butter
2. Margarine
3. Cream
4. Olive oil

Milk:

1. Low fat, skim, dry milk powder

BREAKFAST RECIPES

Blueberry Pancakes

Serves 12 persons

Cooking Time

40 minutes

Ingredients

Cornstarch: ¾ cup

Baking powder: 1 tsp

Butter: 15g

Low fat Milk: 500 ml

Egg: 1

Chopped banana: 1

Blueberries: for garnish

Preparation Method

1. Whisk melted butter into egg and milk.
2. Mix cornstarch and baking powder in separate bowl, and stir in the milk mixture. Keep the mixture lumpy.
3. Mix in the banana and refrigerate the mixture for 30 minutes.
4. Spoon mixture into a non-stick frying pan covered with very light oil and sprinkle with blueberries.
5. Cook the pancake for 3 minutes and then turn over for 2 minutes approximately.
6. Repeat the steps for cooking until the batter is finished.
7. Serve immediately!

Nutritional Value per Serving

Calories: 108kcal

Fat: 3g

Protein: 4g

Carbohydrates: 18g

Mushroom Frittata

Serves 6 persons

Cooking Time

1-hour total

Ingredients

For wild rice:

Water: 2 cups

Wild rice: ½ cup

Salt: 1/8 tsp

Frittata:

Eggs: 5 large

Egg whites: 2

Parsley: 2 tbsp

Salt: 1 tsp

Ground pepper: ½ tsp

Ground nutmeg: ¼ tsp

Olive oil: 2 tsp

Red onions: 1 cup (chopped)

Minced rosemary: 1 tbsp

Mixed mushrooms: 1 pound (cremini, white button, shiitake)

Parmesan cheese: ½ cup (shredded)

Chopped prosciutto: 4 slices

Preparation Method

1. Combine water, rice, and salt in small pan to prepare wild rice. Bring to boil and cover, let it cook on low heat for 30-40 minutes.
2. Beat eggs and egg whites in large bowl with parsley, ¼ tsp salt, ¼ tsp pepper, and nutmeg while rice is cooking to prepare the frittata.
3. Heat oil in ovenproof skillet, add onion, ¼ tsp salt, and pepper, and cook. Stir in rosemary after 3 minutes and add mushrooms, stir frequently. Stir in rice after 8 minutes and reduce heat.
4. Pour egg mixture over rice and vegetables, cover and cook for about 5 minutes.
5. Sprinkle with parmesan cheese and prosciutto and serve warm
6. Note: to prepare this recipe quickly, prepare rice the night before or use rice leftovers from before.

Nutritional Value per Serving

Calories: 155

Fat: 11g

Protein: 11g

Carbohydrates: 3g

Potato Waffles

Serves 10-12 persons

Cooking Time

15 minutes

Ingredients

Potato flakes: 45g

Potato flour: 45 g

Brown rice flour: 45 g

Grated parmesan: 3 tbsp

Salt: 1/8 tsp

Chipotle chili pepper: a pinch

Baking powder: ½ tsp

Unsweetened almond milk: 280 ml

Eggs: 3 (beaten)

Preparation Method

1. Mix potato flakes, potato, and cheese, salt, baking powder, and rice flour in a bowl.
2. Add heated almond milk and eggs to dry ingredients and mix well.
3. Spoon batter into a waffle maker and make sure not to overfill.
4. Cook waffles until they are crisp on the outside. It should take from 8-10 minutes.
5. Serve immediately.

Nutritional Value per Serving

Calories: 570

Fat: 25g

Protein: 38g

Carbohydrates: 54g

Chicken Apple Sausage

Makes 8 patties

Cooking Time

45 minutes

Ingredients

Olive oil: 2 tsp

Diced onion: 1 small

Apple: 1 (peeled and diced)

Fresh sage: 1 tbsp (chopped)

Chicken: 1 pound

Brown sugar: 1 tbsp

Fennel seed: ½ tsp (chopped)

Salt: ¾ tsp

Pepper: ¼ tsp

Preparation Method

1. Cook onion for 2 minutes in oil over medium heat in skillet. Add apples and cook for further 2 minutes, transfer to bowl and let it cool.
2. Mix chicken, sage, sugar, fennel, salt, and pepper to the apple and onion mixture.
3. Coat pan with cooking spray, and scoop 4 portions of the mixture into pan. Flatten each patty and cook until brown.
4. Serve warm.

Nutritional Value per Serving

Calories: 112

Fat: 6g

Protein: 10g

Carbohydrates: 5g

Onion Frittata

Serves one person

Cooking Time

10 minutes

Ingredients

Diced onion: 1 cup

Water: ¼ cup + 1 tbsp

Olive oil: 1 tsp

Eggs: 2 (beaten)

Chopped herbs: 2 tsp

Salt: 1/8 tsp

Pepper: 1/8 tsp

Preparation Method

1. Place a non-skillet pan over medium high heat, and boil ¼-cup water and onions. Cover and cook for 2 minutes or until water has evaporated. Drizzle in oil, and brown onions.
2. Add egg mixture and stir constantly.
3. Reduce heat and sprinkle with herbs, salt, and pepper. Spoon cheese on top and cook for 2 minutes or until cheese is set and egg is cooked.
4. Serve hot.

Nutritional Value per Serving

Calories: 110

Fat: 10g

Protein: 9g

Carbohydrates: 17g

Spanish omelet

Serves 3-4 persons

Cooking Time

30 minutes

Ingredients

Potatoes: 500g

Butter: one knob

Sliced onion: 2 small

Red pepper: 1 (chopped)

Eggs: 8-9

Salt and pepper: to taste

Preparation Method

1. Cut the potatoes into small slices and finely chop the onions and red pepper
2. Heat butter and cook gently for 10 minutes over low heat. Add peppers when it starts to brown and cook for 5 more minutes.
3. Steam potatoes in boiling water until soft.
4. Beat eggs with salt and pepper.
5. Pour egg mixture in frying pan over butter and potatoes. Cook until set for almost 15 minutes.
6. Serve hot!

Nutritional Value per Serving

Calories: 516 kcal

Fat: 43g

Protein: 12g

Carbohydrates: 23g

Raspberry Avocado Smoothie

Serves 2 persons

Cooking Time

5 minutes

Ingredients

Avocado: 1

Orange juice: ¾ cup

Frozen raspberries: ½ cup

Preparation Method

1. Puree all ingredients in blender, and blender until smooth.

Nutritional Value per Serving

Calories: 249

Fat: 14g

Protein: 3g

Carbohydrates: 32g

Crispy Potatoes with Beans and Eggs

Serves 4 persons

Cooking Time

40 minutes

Ingredients

Cooked green beans: 1 cup

Olive oil: 2 tbsp

Diced cooked potatoes: 5 cups

Minced garlic: 2 cloves

Crushed red pepper: 1/8 tsp

Salt: ½ tsp

Ground pepper: to taste

Eggs: 4

Preparation Method

1. Heat oil over medium heat, spread potatoes and cook until tender and brown, about 15 minutes. Stir in garlic, green beans, salt, pepper, and crushed red pepper.
2. One by one crack each egg into the pan, on top of vegetables, spacing evenly. Cover and cook the eggs to your taste or until the whites are set and the yolk is cooked.
3. Serve immediately.

Nutritional Value per Serving

Calories: 315

Fat: 12g

Protein: 10g

Carbohydrates: 42g

Maple Cinnamon Applesauce

Serves 1-2 persons

Cooking Time

40 minutes

Ingredients

Peeled McIntosh apples: 6 (cut into pieces)

Golden delicious or other sweet apple: 2 (cut into pieces)

Water: ¼ cup

Maple syrup: 2 tbsp

Cinnamon: ½ tsp

Preparation Method

1. In a large saucepan, combine apple pieces and water. After it comes to a boil, reduce heat, cover, and let it cook. Stir once or twice until apples are soft, about 30 minutes.
2. Mash apples when soft, stir in maple syrup and cinnamon.
3. Serve in a colorful bowl.

Note: This recipe can be refrigerated for up to 2 weeks or frozen up to 6 months.

Nutritional Value per Serving

Calories: 77

Fat: 0g

Protein: 0g

Carbohydrates: 20g

Banana Pancakes

Makes 16 pancakes

Cooking Time

20 minutes

Ingredients

Eggs: 2 large

Melted butter: 1 ½ tsp

Milk: 1/2 cup

Banana: 1

Gluten free baking powder: 1 tbsp

Rice flour: 1 cup

Extra butter to fry pancakes

Preparation Method

1. Process all liquid ingredients in a food processor and slowly add the gluten free baking powder, banana and rice flour. Process until smooth.
2. Heat frying pan over medium heat. Let a tsp of butter sizzle in pan and then pour the batter until it becomes approximately 2 inches in diameter.
3. Turn pancakes when bubbles come to top, continue to fry until golden brown.
4. Take the pancake down and place in warm oven until all pancakes are made.
5. Serve hot.

Nutritional Value per Serving

Calories: 195 kcal

Fat: 7g

Protein: 5g

Carbohydrates: 30g

LUNCH RECIPES

Quinoa and Feta Salad with Roasted Vegetables

Serves 4 persons

Cooking Time

30 minutes

Ingredients

Quinoa: 200g

Olive oil: 3 tbsp

Red onion: 1 (cut into round slices)

Red, yellow or a mixture of pepper: 2 (cut into chunky wedges and deseeded)

Baby courgettes: 200g (halved lengthwise)

Garlic cloves: 3 (unpeeled)

Lemon: 1 (zest and juice)

Sugar: a pinch

Parsley: one small pack (roughly chopped)

Feta cheese: 200g pack

Preparation Method

1. Cook quinoa and set aside.
2. Heat oven to 200C/180C fan/gas and toss onions and peppers in 1 tbsp of oil in roasting tray. Roast for 15 minutes.
3. With the rest of the vegetables toss courgettes and garlic and roast for 15 more minutes.
4. Mash the roasted garlic cloves without skin. Stir in remaining lemon juice, oil, zest, and sugar. Drizzle it over the quinoa. Combine vegetables and parsley with quinoa and toss well.
5. Serve with feta cheese crumbled on top.

Nutritional Value per Serving

Calories: 404kcal

Fat: 22g

Protein: 18g

Carbohydrates: 36g

Rice Noodles with Sundried Tomatoes, Basil and Parmesan

Serves 4 persons

Cooking Time

10 minutes

Ingredients

Rice noodles: 250g

Garlic cloves: 3

Sundried tomatoes: 85g

Parmesan cheese: 25g

Basil leaves: a handful

Preparation Method

1. Prepare the noodles, drain, and set aside.
2. Fry tomatoes and garlic in oil over medium heat for 3 minutes.
3. Toss noodles, cheese, and basil into the pan and mix well.
4. Serve immediately.

Nutritional Value per Serving

Calories: 329 kcal

Fat: 10g

Protein: 7g

Carbohydrates: 55g

Corn Tortilla Crusted Chicken

Serves 4 persons

Cooking Time

35 minutes

Ingredients

Roughly torn corn tortillas: 10

Cornstarch: ¼ cup

Buttermilk: 1 cup

Chicken tenders: 12

Olive oil: 2 cups

Grainy mustard: 3 tbsp

Honey: 3 tbsp

Salt and pepper: to taste

Preparation Method

1. Pulse tortillas in food processor until course. Transfer to bowl and season with salt and pepper. Put cornstarch in plate and pour buttermilk in a shallow dish.
2. Cover chicken in cornstarch, shaking off excess and then coat in buttermilk. Dredge in tortilla crumbs and transfer to baking sheet.
3. Heat oil over medium heat. Cook chicken in two batches until crust becomes golden. It will take about 12 minutes, remember to flip.
4. In a bowl, stir mustard and honey together to make the dip (optional).
5. Serve chicken with dip.

Nutritional Value per Serving

Calories: 550g

Fat: 96g

Protein: 8g

Carbohydrates: 51g

Sweet Potato and Lentil Stew

Serves 6 persons

Cooking Time

1 hour

Ingredients

Olive oil: 2 tbsp

Onion: 1 (chopped)

Carrots: 2 (chopped)

Celery ribs: 2 (chopped)

Bay leaf: 1

Minced garlic clove: 1

Curry powder: 1 ½ tsp

Dried brown lentils: 2 cups

Sweet potatoes: 2 (cut into pieces)

Green beans: 1 pack

Diced tomatoes: 1 can

Cilantro leaves: ½ cup (chopped)

Salt and pepper: to taste

Low fat yoghurt: for serving

Water: 7 cups

Preparation Method

1. Heat oil over medium heat in large saucepan. Cook and soften onions, carrots, celery, and bay leaf in oil. Add curry powder and garlic and cook for 1 minutes or until fragrant.
2. Boil lentils in water and bring to a boil. Cover and cook for ten minutes after reducing heat. Continue to cook after adding potatoes (15 minutes) or until potatoes are tender.
3. Cook a further 4 minutes by adding green beans and tomatoes. Add cilantro, season with salt and pepper.
4. Serve with yoghurt.

Nutritional Value per Serving

Calories: 199

Fat: 2g

Protein: 11g

Carbohydrates: 35g

Papaya Shrimp and Soba Salad

Served 4

Cooking Time

30 minutes

Ingredients

Soba noodles: 8 ounces

Tamarind concentrate: 1/3 cup

Light brown sugar: 2 tbsp

Olive oil: ¼ cup

Fresh lime juice: 1 tbsp

Cayenne pepper: ½ tsp

Fresh cilantro leaves: 1 cup

Sliced red onion: 1

Sliced papaya: 1

Chopped salted peanuts: ½ cup

Shrimp: 1 pound

Ground coriander: ½ tsp

Salt and pepper: to taste

Preparation Method

1. Cook soba noodles in a large pot of boiling salted water and set aside.
2. Whisk together tamarind, sugar, lime juice, 2 tbsp oil and cayenne in a large pot. Add cilantro, noodles, onion, half the papaya, and 3 tbsp of peanuts. Add salt, pepper to taste, and combine well.
3. Heat 2 tbsp of oil in a large skillet, add garlic, and cook until brown. Set aside garlic, raise the heat, and add shrimp. Sprinkle with coriander, salt, and pepper. Cook for about 3 minutes, tossing occasionally.
4. Serve hot.

Nutritional Value per Serving:

Calories: 270

Fat: 1g

Protein: 10g

Carbohydrates: 63g

Oven Puttanesca

Serves 6 persons

Cooking Time

50 minutes

Ingredients

Tomatoes: 6 (cut into wedges)

Thinly sliced garlic cloves: 2

Capers: 3 tbsp

Olive oil: 2 tbsp

Salt and pepper: to taste

Kalamata olives: 1/3 cup

Gluten free penne: 12 ounces

Preparation Method

1. Preheat oven to 425 degrees.
2. On a rimmed baking sheet, toss tomatoes, garlic, capers, oil, salt, and pepper. Roast for 35 minutes and reduce oven to 375 degrees. Add olives and roast for 15 more minutes.
3. In the meantime, cook the pasta and set aside.
4. Toss the pasta with tomato sauce and serve warm.

Nutritional Value per Serving

Calories: 73

Fat: 6g

Protein: 2g

Carbohydrates: 6g

DINNER RECIPES

Curried Rice with Shrimp

Serves 4

Cooking Time

40 minutes

Ingredients

Olive oil: 1 tbsp

Chopped onion: 1

Chopped carrots: 2

Chopped garlic cloves: 2

Curry powder: 2 tsp

White rice: 1 cup

Salt and pepper: to taste

Shrimps: 1 ½ pound

Fresh basil: ½ cup

Preparation Method

1. Cook onions and carrots over medium heat, until soft.
2. Stir in garlic and curry powder, cook for 2 minutes.
3. Add 2 ½ cups water, rice and ½ tsp salt and pepper and bring to boil. Reduce heat and cover, for 15 minutes.
4. Take ½ tsp salt and ¼ tsp pepper and season the shrimps. Nestle them in partially cooked rice. Cover and cook for about 5 more minutes. Serve immediately with basil.

Nutritional Value per Serving

Calories: 431

Fat: 7g

Protein: 39g

Carbohydrates: 50g

Tuna with Black Pepper and Lemon

Serves 4

Cooking Time

30 minutes

Ingredients

Rice: 1 cup

Olive oil: 2 tbsp

Red onion: ½

Artichoke hearts: 3 6.5-ounce jars

Lemon: 1 (cut into 8 slices)

Garlic cloves: 2

Fresh tuna: 1 ½ pounds (cut in cubes)

Kosher salt: 1 ½ tsp

Black pepper: 1 tsp

Preparation Method

1. Cook rice and set aside.
2. Place a skillet over medium heat and pour 1 tbsp of oil. Cook onion for about 3 minutes in skillet.
3. Add lemon, garlic, and artichoke hearts until heated through and transfer to plate.
4. Season tuna with salt, pepper, and heat remaining oil in skillet.
5. Cook tuna until brown on all sides. Toss the artichoke mixture back in skillet and serve over with rice.

Nutritional Value per Serving

Calories: 390

Fat: 15g

Protein: 44g

Carbohydrates: 22g

Chicken with Tomatoes and White Beans

Serves 4

Cooking Time

50 minutes

Ingredients

Grape tomatoes: 1 pint

Fresh thyme: 4 sprigs

Cannellini beans: 2 15.5-ounce cans

Fresh oregano: 4 sprigs

Olive oil: 2 tbsp

Garlic cloves: 2

Crushed red pepper: ¼ tsp

Black pepper and kosher salt: to taste

Chicken thighs: 8

Preparation Method

1. Heat oven to 425 degree F. toss beans, tomatoes, thyme and oregano sprigs, red pepper, garlic, 1 tbsp oil, ¼ tsp black pepper and ½ tsp salt in a large baking dish.
2. Season chicken with ½ tsp salt, ¼ tsp black pepper and rub with remaining oil. Place on top of beans mixture.
3. Roast until chicken is golden and cooked for about 40 minutes. Sprinkle with oregano leaves and serve.

Nutritional Value per Serving

Calories: 600

Fat: 35g

Protein: 51g

Carbohydrates: 22g

Turkey and Pablano Chili

Serves 4

Cooking Time

40 minutes

Ingredients

Olive oil: 1 tbsp

Chopped poblano pepper: 1

Chopped onion: 1

Cumin: 2 tsp

Diced tomatoes: 1 28-ounce can

Kidney beans: 2 15.5-ounce cans

Black pepper and kosher salt

Roasted turkey or chicken: 2 cups (shredded)

Preparation Method

1. In a large saucepan, heat oil over medium high heat.
2. Cook onion and poblano until soften and add cumin, tomatoes, beans, 2-cup water, 1 ¼ tsp salt, and ¼ tsp pepper and bring to boil.
3. Stir occasionally and reduce heat. Cook for 12-15 minutes, until slightly thickened.
4. Add turkey and cook for about 3 minutes.

Nutritional Value per Serving

Calories: 700

Fat: 17g

Protein: 53g

Carbohydrates: 93g

Cumin Chicken with Black Beans

Serves 4

Cooking Time

25 minutes

Ingredients

Boneless chicken breast: 2

Cumin: ¼ tsp

Cayenne pepper: ¼ tsp

Olive oil: 2 tbsp

Red onion: ½ cup (chopped)

Jalapeno pepper: 1 (chopped)

Black beans: 3 cups

Corn kernels: 1 ½ cup

Cilantro: 2 tbsp

Red wine vinegar: 2 tsp

Black pepper

Kosher salt

Preparation Method

1. Pound chicken with mallet to ½-inch thickness by placing between 2 sheets of plastic wrap. Rub the chicken with cumin and cayenne.
2. Heat oil over medium heat and sauté chicken for 4 minutes each side and transfer to cutting board.
3. Cook jalapeno and onion for a minute in skillet, add beans, corn, tomatoes, 3 tbsp water and cook for 3 minutes, stirring occasionally.
4. Toss the chicken with scallions, cilantro, and vinegar. Season with salt and pepper and arrange on beans. Serve hot.

Nutritional Value per Serving

Calories: 324

Fat: 9g

Protein: less than one g

Carbohydrates: 45g

Chicken Risotto

Serves 2-3 persons

Cooking Time

35 minutes

Ingredients

Risotto rice: 200g

Olive oil: 2 tbsp+1 tbsp

Chopped onion: 1

Chopped red pepper: 1

Chopped green pepper: 1

Sliced mushrooms: 10-12

Wheat free chicken stock: 750 ml

Chopped chicken breasts: 2-3

Dried oregano: 2 tsp

Black pepper

Preparation Method

1. Add risotto rice to 2 tbsp oil and heat for 2-3 minutes.
2. Add peppers, onion, and mushrooms and cook for 5 minutes. Take care not to brown the rice.
3. Add stock and bring to boil. Reduce heat and simmer for 25 minutes approximately, uncovered. Make sure rice becomes tender, and add more water if necessary.
4. Cook chicken pieces in 1 tbsp oil until lightly browned.
5. In the end, mix chicken, oregano and seasoning well.
6. Serve immediately.

Nutritional Value per Serving

Calories: 785 kcal

Fat: 33g

Protein: 56g

Carbohydrates: 68g

Printed in Great Britain
by Amazon

62870919R00031